GEMINI:

A COMPLETE GUIDE TO THE GEMINI ASTROLOGY STAR SIGN

Sofia Visconti

Contents

INTRODUCTION

For centuries astrology has captured the imagination of humanity. A canvas where stars and planets intertwine to tell the tales of our existence. At its core astrology explores the movements and positions of celestial bodies. From this it explores their impact on our affairs and the world. This ancient practice transcends time and cultures by offering insights into personality traits, relationships, life events and much more.

The essence of astrology lies in the belief that an individual's character and destiny are shaped by the alignment of stars and planets at the moment of their birth. Each zodiac sign corresponds to a period within a year. Each carries distinct characteristics and attributes. The twelve signs form a belt encircling the sky, are divided into segments named after their respective constellations.

In this book we delve into one constellation, Gemini. Our journey, through these pages, aims to unravel the qualities, characteristics and background of those born under the influence of Gemini's star sign. The purpose of this book is to serve as a guide for Geminis who want to gain self awareness and for those who wish to understand the Geminis in their lives. Whether you are a Gemini yourself or have a connection with one. This book will offer insights into the strengths, challenges and potentials associated with this zodiac sign.

OVERVIEW OF GEMINI

- **Date**; May 21st - June 20th. This period marks the transition from spring to summer in the Northern Hemisphere. This is a time, associated with the blossoming of ideas and the joy of learning.
- **Symbol**; The symbol of Gemini is the Twins, which represents the duality inherent in this sign.
- **Element**; Gemini is an Air sign. Air signs are characterized by their intellectual, communicative and analytical abilities.
- **Planet**; Mercury, the planet associated with intellect, communication skills and agility.

- **Color**; Yellow represents energy, a positive outlook and an open mind.
- **Traits**; Individuals born under Gemini are renowned for their agile nature, sociability and intelligence.

STRENGTHS

- **Adaptability**; Geminis are skilled at adapting to various situations.
- **Communication Skills**; They excel in expressing themselves and understanding others.
- **Intellect**; Geminis naturally gravitate towards learning and exploring intellectual concepts.
- **Sociability**; They are individuals who thrive on social interactions.

WEAKNESSES

- **Indecisiveness**; Geminis can find it challenging to make decisions due to their indecisive nature.
- **Impulsiveness**; Their curiosity sometimes leads them to act without thought.
- **Inconsistency**; Their diverse range of interests can result in a lack of focus at times.
- **Compatibility**; Geminis generally get along well with air signs (Libra, Aquarius) and fire signs (Aries, Leo, Sagittarius) as they share similar energy and perspectives on life.

In our introduction we explored the captivating world of the Gemini star sign offering an exploration of its multifaceted nature. It begins by placing Gemini within the context of astrology, emphasizing how celestial bodies have long been believed to influence lives. Subsequent chapters in the book promise an in depth exploration of Gemini. By combining insights, practical tips and captivating narratives this book aims to offer an accessible guide for comprehending and appreciating the complexities as well, as the allure of the Gemini zodiac sign.

CHAPTER 1: HISTORY AND MYTHOLOGY

In this chapter we will explore the history and mythological origins of Gemini. This exploration will not only deepen our understanding of Gemini, it will also shed light on the profound influence that celestial events have had on humanity. The constellation of Gemini has captivated people, across cultures and time. Let's embark on a journey through history and mythology to uncover the stories behind this sign.

We will begin by examining how ancient civilizations observed and documented Gemini. From the ancient gods in Mesopotamia to Greek and Roman mythology, each tale reflects both the astronomical knowledge and the cultural beliefs of those times. As we move forward in time we will discover how various cultures interpreted and depicted Gemini in their star maps. These interpretations offer a range of meanings for the twins. From being protectors and patrons, to representing duality, intelligence and communication.

This chapter not only provides an overview but also immerses us in captivating mythological narratives that have shaped our understanding of Gemini. We will encounter figures associated with this zodiac sign whose stories echo themes of brotherhood, intellect and adaptability. Come along with us on this journey as we unveil the secrets and legends surrounding Gemini. A sign that has fascinated humans for centuries.

EARLIEST OBSERVATIONS IN ANCIENT CIVILIZATIONS

MESOPOTAMIA

The Mesopotamians were among the first to record and associate the Gemini constellation with the Great Twins, Gilgamesh and Enkidu. These twins held a significance in star mythology. They were protectors. This association highlights the Geminis themes of duality and finding balance.

ANCIENT GREECE

Moving to Ancient Greece, Gemini was linked to the twin brothers Castor and Pollux collectively known as the Dioscuri. They were regarded as patrons of sailors symbolizing both brotherhood and navigation. When Castor tragically lost his life Pollux felt grief. He pleaded with Zeus to grant him immortality so that he could be reunited with his twin. Touched by this display of love Zeus immortalized them both as the constellation Gemini, in the night sky. This tale beautifully portrays themes of brotherhood, loyalty and an unbreakable bond that transcends death. All deeply resonating with the relational connection associated with Gemini.

ANCIENT ROME

The ancient Romans followed suit by incorporating Gemini into their lore. They associated this constellation with Romulus and Remus, founders of Rome. Together they represent the city's beginnings and divine protection. The Romans revered them as protectors of the city. Throughout times of war and conflict people often turned to the concept of unity and cooperation as a symbol of strength.

CHINESE ASTRONOMY

Chinese astronomy integrated the stars of Gemini into constellations within their own system. One notable example is their inclusion in the White Tiger of the West formation. Unlike other interpretations centered around twins, Chinese cosmology offered a new perspective on these stars.

INDIA ASTRONOMY

In the astronomy of India, the stars of Gemini were viewed as a pair of physicians known as Ashvins who served as gods. They were regarded as symbols of good health, fortune, rejuvenation and healing.

INDIGENOUS CULTURES

Indigenous cultures also had their own interpretations of the stars within the Gemini constellation. For instance in American traditions these stars might have been seen as a pair of animals or other significant figures from their cultural stories and mythologies.

Across the cultures mentioned above, it is evident that the Gemini constellation consistently represents concepts such as duality, connection and transformation. Whether portrayed as brothers or celestial twins, or even protective deities themselves; the Gemini constellation has always been more than two stars, in the night sky. It has been a reflection that mirrors the intricate complexities and dualities embedded within human experiences.

The historical journey of the Gemini constellation demonstrates how various cultures throughout time have gazed upon the stars and deciphered their own narratives. Whether depicting twins, celestial patrons or symbols of healing, how Gemini is represented on star maps and in folklore reflects the tapestry of human culture and its profound connection with the universe.

From ancient times to the Middle Ages the concept of Gemini was surrounded by stories often portrayed as twins or brothers in different cultures. This symbolism was closely associated with ideas of duality, brotherhood and the transition between spring and summer.

As the Renaissance and Enlightenment periods unfolded our understanding of astronomy deepened. However astrological interpretations of Gemini still heavily relied on celestial symbols. In the modern era astrology has taken a psychological approach. Contemporary discussions about Gemini often focus on agility, communication skills and its ability to adapt to situations, highlighting its dual nature. This shift from mythological to interpretations is representative of a trend in astrology. It has evolved from a myth based practice into an introspective and therapeutic tool that helps explore personality traits, identity formation and human relationships.

HISTORICAL EVENTS UNDER THE GEMINI SIGN

Gemini season has witnessed many events throughout history. These occurrences are often interpreted in astrology as reflections of Gemini's qualities of adaptability, communication and intellect. Below are some notable historical events during Gemini season

- **Advancements in Science**; Many crucial scientific discoveries and events have taken place during the Gemini season. These align with Gemini's association with intelligence and curiosity. For instance we can mention the telegraph communication by Samuel Morse on May 24 1844 and the historic launch of Valentina Tereshkova as the first woman in space on June 16 1963.
- **Political Milestones**; Gemini has also witnessed political events that mirror it's adaptable nature and duality. This period has seen the signing of treaties and declarations including the adoption of the Magna Carta on June 15 1215.
- **Historical Figures Born Under Gemini;** Gemini has given birth to notable figures such as John F. Kennedy (born on May 29 1917) Marilyn Monroe (born on June 1 1926) and Anne Frank (born on June 12 1929). Their impact on society and culture resonates with the multifaceted nature associated with Gemini traits. In addition brilliant

scientific thinkers, such as Alan Turing (born on June 23 1912) are often linked to the Gemini trait of having an intellect.

As we wrap up this chapter we reflect on the captivating collection of stories, myths and historical accounts associated with the Gemini constellation. From the ancient Greeks and Romans, to civilizations like Mesopotamia and beyond. Gemini has symbolized duality, connection and transformation. These cultures showcase the depth and complexity of human relationships as well as our dualistic nature.

FURTHER READING AND REFERENCES

For those interested in exploring the history and mythology of Gemini in greater detail, the following sources offer a wealth of information.

Primary Ancient Texts

- "Theogony" by Hesiod: Provides insight into early Greek mythology, including the story of Castor and Pollux.
- "Metamorphoses" by Ovid: A classical source that explores various Greek and Roman myths, including those associated with the Gemini constellation.

Astronomical and Astrological Texts

- "Almagest" by Ptolemy: An ancient Greek text on astronomy, offering early observations of the Gemini constellation.

- "Brihat Samhita" by Varahamihira: An influential work in Indian astrology, which includes references to the Ashvins and Vedic interpretations of Gemini.

Modern Astrological Writings

- "The Only Astrology Book You'll Ever Need" by Joanna Martine Woolfolk: A contemporary guide that provides insights into modern interpretations of Gemini.
- "Parker's Astrology" by Julia and Derek Parker: A comprehensive guide to astrology, offering a detailed look at the Gemini sign and its traits.
- "Astrology & Numerology" by Sofia Visconti offers a fresh perspective on Astrology and Numerology.

Cultural and Mythological Studies

- "The Greek Myths" by Robert Graves: A detailed exploration of Greek mythology, offering context and stories related to the Gemini constellation.
- "Mythology: Timeless Tales of Gods and Heroes" by Edith Hamilton: A classic text that covers a wide range of myths, including those associated with Gemini.

These sources, ranging from ancient texts to modern interpretations, offer a deeper understanding of the Gemini constellation and its place in both historical and contemporary astrology. Through them, readers can continue to explore the fascinating and multifaceted world of Gemini.

CHAPTER 2: LOVE & COMPATIBILITY

In this chapter we will embark on a journey to explore how the Gemini sign navigates the realms of romance. Geminis are known for their deep thinking, communication skills and a love for variety. All of which bring a unique and dynamic flavor to their romantic experiences. As we delve into this chapter we will uncover the characteristics that define how Geminis approach love. We will discuss their preference for meaningful connections, playful banter and their deep seated need for understanding. By exploring these traits we will gain insights into how they shape their interactions with their partners.

Compatibility plays an important role in a Gemini's love life. We will also examine which zodiac signs harmonize best with Gemini's versatile nature. This exploration will reveal the complexities of compatibility while highlighting the synergy between Gemini individuals and potential partners. Furthermore we will discuss both the challenges and triumphs that Geminis encounter in their quest for love.

Overall our goal in this chapter is to offer an understanding of how Geminis romantic inclinations align with the stars. Whether you're a Gemini seeking insights into your love life or someone interested in forming a bond with a Gemini. This exploration will provide perspectives on love, relationships and astrological compatibility. Join us as we explore the dynamic world of love and compatibility for Geminis.

GEMINI'S LOVE AND COMPATIBILITY WITH OTHER ZODIAC SIGNS

GEMINI AND ARIES

Aries and Gemini usually have a lively relationship. Aries brings passion and determination which aligns well with Gemini's love for stimulation and social interaction. Both signs value their independence creating a balanced partnership.

However sometimes Aries impulsiveness may clash with Gemini's tendency to be indecisive. Effective communication becomes essential in navigating these differences.

GEMINI AND TAURUS

Taurus offers stability and a practical perspective, which can both ground and occasionally frustrate the adventurous Gemini. The intellectual curiosity of Gemini may sometimes clash with Tauruss preference for routine. Differences in energy levels and interests can pose obstacles that require compromise and understanding from both sides.

GEMINI AND GEMINI

When two Geminis come together they often engage in stimulating conversations and enjoy activities together. They recognize each other's need for personal space and variety. Their similar qualities enhance the relationships energy levels and foster creativity. However their shared tendency, towards inconsistency or lack of focus might lead to instability if not properly managed.

GEMINI AND CANCER

Cancer's depth of emotions can bring warmth to Gemini. However conflicts may arise due to Gemini's love for freedom and variety conflicting with Cancers desire for security and stability in relationships. There may be instances of miscommunication that require Gemini to be more empathetic while Cancer needs to understand Gemini's need for expression.

GEMINI AND LEO

Leo's charismatic and lively personality blends well with Gemini's communicative nature. Both enjoy being in the limelight leading to a fun filled and dynamic relationship of excitement and adventure. It is important for them to ensure that they share the spotlight equally as both signs thrive on attention.

GEMINI AND VIRGO

Both signs are ruled by Mercury. These signs share a love for creative pursuits. However there might be clashes between Virgo's attention to detail and Gemini's broader range of interests. A flourishing and happy relationship requires respect and understanding between the two.

GEMINI AND LIBRA

Compatibility is high between these two, as both are air signs. Gemini and Libra naturally connect through their shared affinity for communication and social interaction. Naturally this makes for a great relationship. Keep building upon their strengths and a lasting love is guaranteed.

GEMINI AND SCORPIO

Compatibility is not the best. But it is not the worst either. Gemini might find Scorpios intensity and depth intriguing. Sometimes it can be a bit overwhelming. Scorpio on the hand might see Gemini's lightheartedness, as being a bit superficial. Building trust and emotional depth requires effort. Scorpio needs connection while Gemini values their freedom.

GEMINI AND SAGITTARIUS

Both signs share a love for adventure, learning and exploration. Sagittarius' philosophical approach to life complements Gemini's curiosity leading to an expanding relationship. They both need to strike a balance between independence and commitment in order to maintain a relationship.

GEMINI AND CAPRICORN

Not the best match but there is always potential for these two. Capricorn's practicality and ambition can add

structure to Gemini's diverse ideas. However Capricorn's serious nature may clash with Gemini. It is important for them to understand and respect each other's approaches to life and goals in order to create harmony.

GEMINI AND AQUARIUS

Being both air signs there is an understanding and connection between Gemini and Aquarius. Aquarius' innovative ideas complement Gemini's curiosity leading to a forward thinking partnership. Since both signs value their independence, establishing a grounded relationship can present a challenge.

GEMINI AND PISCES

Pisces brings depth and emotional insight to the partnership with Gemini. Meanwhile Gemini adds depth and intellectual stimulation to Pisces. This combination can be enriching yet also pose challenges. The emotional sensitivity of Pisces may overwhelm Gemini at times while Gemini's rational approach might perplex Pisces. Emotional understanding and effective communication are crucial for navigating these differences.

TIPS FOR RELATIONSHIPS WITH GEMINI

Dating a Gemini whether it's a man or a woman can be an exhilarating and intellectually stimulating experience. Geminis are known for their wit, curiosity and dynamic personalities, which bring excitement and diversity to relationships. Here are some personalized tips for dating and maintaining relationships with Gemini individuals.

- **Engage His Mind**; Have engaging conversations that stimulate his intellect. Share your thoughts. Be open to discussing any topics. Gemini men enjoy having a partner who can keep up with their quick thinking.

- **Embrace Adventure**; Gemini men often crave variety and excitement. Be open to new experiences and adventures together. This will keep the relationship vibrant and captivating for them.

- **Respect His Independence;** Gemini men highly value their freedom. It's crucial to respect their need for space and independence without taking it. Trust them. Give them the room to be themselves.

- **Adaptability;** Remain flexible as Gemini men can be unpredictable at times frequently changing their minds. Being adaptable is essential in maintaining harmony in the relationship.

- **Share Laughter;** A good sense of humor is an excellent way to connect with a Gemini man. Heartedness and playful banter can make your time together more enjoyable.

- **Avoid Falling into a Monotonous Routine;** It's important to steer away from getting stuck in a boring routine. Gemini men thrive on diversity and new experiences so it's essential to keep things varied.

- **Effective Communication is Key;** Gemini women love engaging in conversations and expressing themselves. It's crucial to participate in discussions and actively listen. Building a relationship with a Gemini woman revolves around communication.

- **Appreciate Her Intellectual Abilities;** Show interest in her ideas and thoughts. Gemini women value partners who recognize and appreciate their intellect as those who can engage them in intelligent conversations.

- **Embrace Social Interactions;** Gemini women often enjoy social settings. Be open to attending gatherings and meeting new people.

- **Respect Her Need for Independence;** Just like their male counterparts, Gemini women highly value their independence. Respect her desire for space.

- **Nurture Emotional Connection;** While intellectual compatibility is important it's equally important not to neglect the bond. Despite their independent nature Gemini women also crave emotional connections.

- **Be Patient with Dualities;** Gemini women can have personalities that may seem contradictory, at times. It's important to be patient, understanding and accepting of the facets of her character.

Overall remember it's essential to understand that each individual is unique. The secret to building a connection with a Gemini regardless of gender lies in effective communication and empathy. The key takeaway from this chapter is the significance of communication and flexibility within relationships involving Geminis. Partners who are willing to engage in honest conversations embrace change gracefully and appreciate the nature of Gemini will discover a deeply fulfilling relationship.

Gemini individuals may appear lighthearted and playful, on the surface. However they are capable of forming emotional connections. The challenge for Geminis lies in finding a balance between their nature and their emotions. When they discover a partner who appreciates this duality and creates an environment where both sides can coexist, Geminis can experience fulfilling romantic relationships.

To summarize Geminis approaches love and romance from angles making it an evolving journey. Their relationships thrive on stimulation, effective communication and the desire for both variety and independence. Recognizing and embracing these characteristics can lead to partnerships that stand the test of time.

CHAPTER 3:
FRIENDS AND FAMILY

This chapter explores the friends and family of Geminis. As we delve into the lives of Geminis we uncover the nuances of their interactions with friends and family. Known for their eloquence, adaptability and insatiable curiosity Geminis bring a unique flavor to their relationships. They are great connectors often becoming the life and soul of any gathering. However this same liveliness and love for diversity can occasionally result in inconsistency. Or a hesitation to explore emotional connections.

In terms of friendship Geminis excel as stimulating companions who're always open to ideas and experiences. Nevertheless their need for variety and intellectual stimulation can sometimes clash with the desire for relationships grounded in consistency. Within the family context, Geminis display versatility by taking on roles ranging from peacemakers to problem solvers. However their yearning for space and independence can sometimes create tension with family expectations.

Through insights and observations we will examine Geminis' approaches to their loved ones to harmonize these intricate dynamics. By doing so, we aim to nurture relationships that are fulfilling and long lasting. Join us as we dive into the realm of Gemini;. family and friends.

Together lets unravel the mysteries and embrace the joys that come with these vibrant connections.

GEMINI AS A FRIEND

Having a Gemini as a friend is truly captivating and intriguing. Truly they embody the duality represented by their twins. Here are some key aspects of being friends with a Gemini.

- **Engaging**; Geminis thrive on stimulating discussions delving into topics ranging from scientific breakthroughs to the nuances of various art forms.
- **Social**; Geminis effortlessly navigate social circles. Their ability to mingle and engage with groups makes them exceptional companions at gatherings.
- **Versatile**; Geminis are individuals who easily embrace new situations. Whether it's embarking on an adventure or trying something they make great travel companions for exploring uncharted territories.
- **Inconsistency**; One negative aspect of having a Gemini friend is their inconsistency. They may change plans or flip flop, on opinions. It stems from their curious and exploratory nature.
- **Humor**; Geminis typically possess a fantastic sense of humor. With their sharp wit they effortlessly find humor in situations making them enjoyable and entertaining friends.
- **Empathetic**; They possess an ability to comprehend diverse perspectives making them

empathetic companions who can provide meaningful guidance.

- **Independence**; Geminis highly value their independence. Occasionally they require some time to explore their individual interests. It's important not to mistake this trait for a lack of interest in friendship.

- **Loyal**; Despite their inclination towards variety and change Geminis are loyal friends. Once they establish a bond they are loyal and supportive, willing to go above and beyond to assist their friends.

- **Inquisitive**; A Gemini friend is always eager to learn. They possess an open mind making them wonderful companions for exploring ideas and diverse cultures.

To sum up, a Gemini friend embodies energy, wit and intellect. Their presence brings excitement and diversity to friendships albeit their need for change and stimulation can sometimes present challenges. Understanding and appreciating their nature can lead to a friendship filled with depth.

GEMINI IN FAMILY DYNAMICS

Gemini individuals, known for their caring nature represented by the twins, bring a positive dynamic to family relationships. Let's see how a Gemini might interact within the family.

- **Great Communicators**; Geminis excel in communication. They are usually the ones who keep the dialogue going during family gatherings and can effectively resolve misunderstandings through discussions.

- **Adaptable**; In family dynamics Geminis are highly adaptable. They can effortlessly switch roles acting as mediators, entertainers or advisors based on what the situation calls for.

- **Wide Range of Interests**; With their range of interests Geminis can easily connect with family members on different levels. For instance they may share a love for sports with one sibling while appreciating music with another.

- **Craving Intellectual Stimulation**; Geminis actively encourage discussions and debates on topics which keeps the family atmosphere dynamic and engaging.

- **Inconsistency**; Their moods may fluctuate at times which can be challenging for some family members to understand.
- **Independence**; Geminis value their independence. They tend to encourage the same among their family members. They value the pursuits and independence of each family member showing their support.
- **Playful**; Geminis bring an youthful energy to the family. They often lighten the atmosphere, adding a sprinkle of humor to family interactions.
- **Avoidance**; Geminis may tend to avoid getting emotionally entangled which can sometimes be misunderstood as detachment. It's crucial for family members to acknowledge that this is part of who they are.
- **Flexibility**; They are individuals who willingly adapt to changing dynamics within the family. Whether it's taking charge during times or stepping back to allow others to lead, Geminis can smoothly adjust their roles as needed.

In conclusion Geminis inject vibrancy, effective communication and adaptability into family life. Their desire for stimulation and variety can greatly contribute to a dynamic family environment. However it's important for other family members to understand and accommodate their fluctuating moods and need for space. Embracing these traits can make the familial experience more fulfilling and harmonious.

CHALLENGES IN FRIENDSHIPS AND FAMILY RELATIONS

Gemini presents their own challenges when it comes to friendships and family relationships due to their inherent traits. Understanding these challenges can help Geminis and their loved ones navigate their relationships effectively.

CHALLENGES IN FRIENDSHIPS

- **Unpredictability**; Geminis love for variety and change can sometimes result in random behavior. Friends may find it challenging to keep up with their changing interests and moods which can lead to misunderstandings.
- **Communication Overflow;** While Geminis excel at communication their constant need to share and discuss things can overwhelm some friends who prefer reflective interactions.
- **Fear of Emotional Intensity;** Geminis may shy away from connections or serious conversations, which could be misinterpreted as shallowness or a lack of commitment to the friendship.
- **Distractibility**; Their natural curiosity and desire to explore everything can occasionally make them appear distracted or less fully engaged in the moment, which might mistakenly be seen as disinterest.
- **Indecisiveness;** Geminis have a tendency towards indecisiveness, which might frustrate friends who rely on them for making decisions or providing opinions.

- **Need for Independence;** Geminis highly value their independence, which can sometimes clash with family expectations. For example in close knit families where collective decision making is the norm.

- **Avoidance;** When it comes to family situations Geminis may tend to avoid delving into emotional conversations. This behavior might make them appear empathetic or engaged in family issues.

- **Juggling Multiple Roles;** Gemini's adaptability, in switching between roles within the family dynamic can sometimes lead to feelings of exhaustion or being misunderstood. Family members may not always recognize their efforts to strike a balance between these roles.

- **Unpredictable Mood Swings;** The dual nature of Geminis can result in mood swings that are challenging for family members to comprehend or anticipate. This can create a sense of instability during interactions within the family.

- **Craving Variety versus Routine;** Gemini individuals desire for change and variety may clash with the stability. Routine typically found in family life. Consequently they might experience restlessness or a feeling of being confined.

As we wrap up our exploration of how Geminis interact in the realms of friendship and family it becomes clear that this journey is as diverse and complex as the sign itself. Geminis, with their duality and appreciation for diversity bring an energy to their relationships. However maintaining harmony and depth in these connections requires mindfulness and effort. Lets recap some of the key points.

KEY INSIGHTS RECAP

- **Embrace Open Communication**; Geminis thrive on communication. It's important to encourage honest dialogue during emotionally charged situations. This not only helps misunderstandings but also strengthens trust and understanding.

- **Respect Individuality**; Both friends and family members of Geminis should respect their need for space and independence. Understanding this allows Geminis to feel valued and respected, fostering connections.

- **Patience with Inconsistencies**; Recognizing and accepting the fluctuating interests and moods of Geminis can help prevent conflicts. Patience and empathy play roles in nurturing these relationships.

- **Encourage Emotional Expression**; Geminis may benefit from encouragement to explore their emotions deeply. Creating an environment for expression can deepen the bond between individuals.

- **Find Balance**; Geminis should strive to strike a balance, between engagements and personal time. It is essential for individuals to set aside time, for introspection and self care in order to maintain their well being.

- **Growth mindset**; When it comes to relationships with Geminis there is a potential for growth and learning. Embracing their curiosity and thirst for knowledge can lead to shared experiences that enhance these bonds.

- **Flexibility and adaptability**; These are crucial for both Geminis and their loved ones. Being able to adapt to changing circumstances and accommodate each other's needs is key in maintaining a relationship.

- **Self awareness**; To nurture their relationships Geminis should focus on self awareness and understanding how their nature impacts others. It's important for them to recognize any tendencies towards superficiality or indecisiveness and work on improving those aspects, which can result in fulfilling relationships.

In conclusion the relationships involving Geminis resemble dances of energy, change and adaptability. By embracing the qualities that make Geminis unique while also addressing challenges along the way these relationships have the potential to evolve into lasting connections. Embarking on a journey with a Gemini entails conversations, joyful laughter and valuable opportunities for growth and knowledge. It is an experience that combines enrichment and enlightenment. Enjoy the journey for every step is worth it.

CHAPTER 4:
CAREER AND AMBITIONS

Geminis, known for their duality and intellect, stands apart in the zodiac constellation. This chapter explores the connection between Geminis and their professional lives which are as multifaceted as the sign itself. They bring a combination of adaptability, strong communication skills and curiosity to their work. However these very qualities that propel them forward can also present challenges when it comes to maintaining focus and consistency.

Join us on an exploration of the professional realm of Gemini, where we delve into the impact of astrology, on their career paths and financial behavior. This journey will unveil insights into how this adaptable and intellectually driven zodiac sign can unlock their potential in the professional world.

CAREER PREFERENCES AND PROFESSIONAL ASPIRATIONS

Gemini individuals often exhibit key preferences and ambitions in their lives. Naturally they are influenced by their inherent qualities of adaptability, effective communication skills and intellectual curiosity. Here is a brief overview of the career preferences and aspirations for someone born under the Gemini zodiac sign.

- **Versatile and Diverse Roles**; Geminis thrive in careers that offer a range of tasks and opportunities. They prefer roles that're dynamic allowing them to tackle projects and avoid monotony. In terms of their aspirations They often strive for a range of experiences throughout their career. They may explore roles within the field or even switch careers altogether in order to fulfill their desire for variety.
- **Communication Oriented Jobs**; With their ability to communicate effectively Geminis excel in professions that involve writing, speaking or other forms of communication. Careers in journalism, writing, public relations or broadcasting often appeal to them.
- **Stimulating Environments**; They gravitate towards careers that challenge their intellect and

provide learning opportunities. Roles involving research, analysis or problem solving can be particularly attractive to them.

- **Social Interaction**; Geminis enjoy working in environments where they can interact with groups of people. Careers involving teamwork, networking or public engagement align with their nature. They commonly aspire to communication based roles where they can use their skills to influence, educate or entertain others. This could manifest as becoming a journalist, an author or even establishing themselves as a media personality.

- **Autonomy**; They value flexibility in their work environment. Careers that offer a degree of autonomy along with work hours or the option to work remotely tend to be highly appealing to them.

- **Creative**; Fields that require creativity and innovation such as advertising, graphic design or digital media are particularly attractive to Gemini individuals due to their inclination towards being creative and inventive.

- **Growth**; Continuous learning and personal development play roles in the growth of Geminis. They actively seek out opportunities for training, education and new experiences to keep expanding their knowledge and keeping their minds engaged.

In conclusion Gemini individuals pursue careers that're vibrant, intellectually engaging and provide chances for social engagement. Their career goals are fueled by a craving for diversity, ongoing learning and the urge to express their creativity and thoughts. Thanks to their adaptability and strong communication abilities they excel as professionals who can thrive in various industries and positions.

STRENGTHS IN THE WORKPLACE

Gemini individuals possess a set of strengths that contribute to their success, in professional settings. These strengths are rooted in their ability to adapt, think on their feet and communicate effectively. Let's take a look at the strengths that Geminis bring to their workplaces.

- **Adaptability**; Geminis demonstrate adaptability effortlessly adjusting to changing situations and workplace dynamics. Their flexibility proves invaluable in roles that involve handling shifts or diverse tasks.

- **Strong Communication Skills**; Geminis naturally excel in communication. They have a knack for expressing their thoughts persuasively making them highly effective in roles that involve negotiation, presentations or team coordination.

- **Intellectual Curiosity**; Geminis possess a curiosity that drives them to learn and explore new ideas. This quality proves invaluable in industries characterized by evolution since they thrive on staying up to date with the trends and information.

- **Problem Solving**; Known for their analytical minds Geminis approach problems, from various perspectives and devise innovative solutions. Their ability to think outside the box makes them excellent problem solvers.

- **Social Skill**s; With their social nature Geminis are great at networking. They excel at building and maintaining professional relationships, which can greatly benefit any career.
- **Ability to Handle Multiple Tasks**; Geminis have an impressive talent for multitasking. They can effortlessly manage responsibilities simultaneously without compromising the quality of their work.
- **Enthusiasm and Energy**; Geminis often bring a sense of enthusiasm and vitality to the workplace. Their energetic presence has a motivating and uplifting effect on the team.
- **Versatility**; Thanks to their range of interests and skills Geminis are adaptable employees. They can easily adjust to roles or tasks making them valuable assets in dynamic work environments.
- **Quick Learning**; Gemini individuals possess intellects that enable them to grasp concepts and acquire new skills rapidly. This makes them quick learners who can swiftly adapt to roles or technologies.
- **Effective Team Players**; While they appreciate their independence Geminis also excel as team players. They understand how group dynamics work. Make contributions to collaborative efforts.

In summary Gemini individuals bring together a combination of adaptability, communication skills, creativity and intellectual curiosity. These strengths make them well suited for dynamic work environments that require flexibility, problem solving abilities and effective communication skills. Their aptitude for learning and effective collaboration both as contributors and team players renders them invaluable assets, in any professional environment.

PROFESSIONAL CHALLENGES AND STRATEGIES TO OVERCOME THEM

Gemini individuals will encounter many challenges in their professional journeys. Understanding these challenges and employing strategies can aid Geminis in navigating the realm of work successfully.

CAREER CHALLENGES

- **Inconsistency and Difficulty Maintaining Focus**; Geminis occasionally struggle with maintaining consistency. Their ranging interests may result in a lack of focus on a task or project which can impact productivity and hinder career advancement.
- **Impatience**; Their quick thinking nature can sometimes manifest as impatience in situations that require a methodical and deliberate approach. This impatience can lead to frustration in work environments that emphasize attention to detail and patience.
- **Challenges with Routine**; Geminis often find tasks uninspiring, which can contribute to dissatisfaction in jobs lacking diversity and opportunities for creativity.
- **Taking on too much**; With their enthusiasm and willingness to tackle responsibilities Geminis may

occasionally take on more than they can handle leading to stress and exhaustion.

- **Communication Overload**; Although Geminis are skilled, at communication there may be times when they overwhelm their colleagues or clients with an abundance of information. They might also struggle to listen as they speak.

- **Avoidance of In depth Tasks**; Geminis tend to prefer tasks that offer variety and stay on the surface, which can sometimes hinder their ability to engage deeply with detailed work.

- **Organize**; Geminis can benefit from using tools and techniques that help them prioritize tasks and manage their time effectively. By setting goals and deadlines they can bring structure and focus to their work.

- **Mindfulness and Patience Training**; Practices like mindfulness can assist Geminis in developing patience and the ability to concentrate on the task at hand. These qualities are crucial for long term projects requiring attention to detail.

- **Seek Variety within Structure**; Finding roles that offer a mix of tasks within an environment can satisfy Gemini's need for change while still allowing them to maintain focus. This could involve taking on projects within a job position.

- **Set Realistic Commitments**; It's essential for Geminis to realistically assess their workload and establish boundaries in order to avoid overcommitment. Learning how to say no or delegate tasks when necessary becomes crucial in maintaining balance.

- **Develop Active Listening Skills**; While Geminis excel at expressing themselves, focusing on enhancing their listening skills can make them effective communicators overall transforming them into well rounded professionals.

- **Embrace the Power of Deep Work**; Geminis have the ability to gradually train themselves to engage in work. They can start by setting aside time for these tasks and gradually increasing the duration.

- **Consider Career Flexibility**; Geminis can keep themselves engaged and motivated by exploring careers that offer flexibility, such as freelancing or roles with responsibilities.

To sum up, while Geminis may face challenges in their careers due to their love for variety and quick thinking nature, there are strategies they can implement to overcome these obstacles. By organizing their workload, practicing patience and enhancing their listening skills Geminis can not only navigate their careers successfully but also thrive professionally. They can then leverage their strengths to their advantage and make significant progress in their professional endeavors.

In essence, this chapter illuminates the path for Geminis to transform their potential career challenges into stepping stones for success. With an arsenal of strategies like meticulous organization, cultivated patience, and honed listening skills, Geminis are well-equipped to navigate the professional labyrinth with grace and acumen. By embracing these tactics, they can effectively harness their innate gifts of versatility and quick thinking, paving the way to a flourishing and prosperous career journey that sparkles with the unique Gemini brilliance.

CHAPTER 5:
SELF-IMPROVEMENT

This chapter dives into the world of Gemini exploring the paths and practices that lead to growth and fulfillment. We will delve into how Geminis can harness their strengths like adaptability, quick thinking and social finesse to excel in life. Simultaneously we'll address strategies to overcome their weaknesses such as inconsistency, restlessness and a tendency to avoid emotional commitments.

Join us on a journey of self improvement tailored specifically for those born under the Gemini zodiac sign. This adventure guarantees to be both fulfilling and eye opening as it uncovers the potential for growth and transformation that lies within this captivating astrological symbol.

PERSONAL GROWTH AND SELF-DEVELOPMENT

Personal growth and self-development, for individuals born under the Gemini zodiac sign, represented by the symbol of twins, revolves around embracing their duality and harnessing their strengths. The journey towards growth for Geminis encompasses many important aspects.

- **Embracing Dual Nature**; Geminis often exhibit a mix of sociability and solitude, seriousness and playfulness. Personal growth entails recognizing these opposing qualities and harmoniously integrating them.

- **Self Understanding**; Geminis will greatly benefit from introspection, meditation or journaling to gain an understanding of their multifaceted nature. Exploring their thoughts and emotions can be enlightening.

- **Intellectual Advancement**; Geminis possess a thirst for knowledge. Personal growth is nurtured by pursuing education reading extensively or delving into hobbies and skills.

- **Cultivating diverse experiences**; Broadening perspectives through exposure to various experiences is key. Traveling to new places, attending workshops or immersing oneself in cultures can be highly enriching.

- **Social Development**; While Geminis are famed for their intellectual approach it's important to cultivate emotional depth as well. Practices, like mindfulness or seeking counseling contribute to developing intelligence.

COMMUNICATION SKILLS

- **Improving Listening Skills**; While Geminis are great at expressing themselves they can enhance their communication skills by listening and empathizing with others gaining an understanding of different perspectives.

- **Honest Communication**; It's important for Geminis to work on communicating their needs, boundaries and thoughts in an honest and clear manner. This is crucial for growth.

- **Strengthening Relationships**; Geminis have an opportunity for growth when it comes to building meaningful connections. They can focus on being more present during their interactions and investing in their relationships.

CAREER AND PERSONAL ASPIRATIONS

- **Setting Goals**; Geminis may sometimes struggle with finding a direction due to their range of interests. Setting short term and long term goals can help them focus their energy and stay motivated.
- **Balance**; Learning how to balance ambition with finding contentment in the moment is essential for fulfillment. It's about appreciating the present while striving towards aspirations.

HEALTH AND WELLNESS

- **Exercise and Relaxation**; Engaging in activities and relaxation techniques can aid Geminis in managing their occasionally restless energy. Activities like yoga, meditation or participating in sports can be particularly beneficial.
- **Establishing Routine and Structure**; Despite their preference, for variety establishing a routine in daily or weekly schedules can provide a sense of stability and grounding.

In conclusion Geminis can experience growth by finding a balance between their intellectual curiosity, emotional and social well being and overall health. By embracing their multifaceted nature and prioritizing these aspects of life Geminis have the opportunity to embark on a successful journey of self discovery and personal development.

To make the most of Gemini individuals strengths and address their weaknesses it's important to understand their nature and appreciate their qualities. Geminis have a range of strengths that can be capitalized on while their weaknesses offer chances for growth and development. Let's take a look.

HARNESSING STRENGTHS

- **Leveraging Strong Communication**; Geminis have a talent for communication. They can make the most of this strength by pursuing careers or roles that involve writing, speaking, teaching or negotiation. Their ability to express ideas clearly makes them effective in positions that require persuasion or explanation.

- **Embracing Adaptability**; Gemini's inherent adaptability makes them well suited for dynamic work environments and roles that demand thinking and flexibility. They thrive in situations where they need to adjust to changing circumstances.

- **Nurturing Intellectual Curiosity**; Geminis should embrace their love for learning and exploration. Engaging in education whether through channels or self directed pursuits allows them to stay intellectually stimulated and stay ahead in their respective fields.

- **Maximizing Social Skills**; With their social nature Geminis excel at networking and building relationships. They should seize opportunities to connect with others as this can lead to professional growth.

- **Creative Problem Solving**; Gemini's ability to view things from perspectives gives them an edge in problem solving. They are excellent at finding solutions by considering multiple angles. Gemini individuals can take advantage of this during brainstorming sessions and, in roles that value creative solutions.

OVERCOMING WEAKNESSES

- **Prioritizing Consistency**; One of the hurdles for Geminis is their inclination towards inconsistency. To tackle this they can establish routines. Or set goals to maintain focus. Utilizing tools such as planners and to do lists can also be helpful in ensuring consistency in both professional aspects of their lives.
- **Cultivating Patience**; Geminis tend to have a high level of impatience. Engaging in mindfulness practices and exercises that build patience can prove beneficial for them. It's important for them to be present and fully engaged in the moment especially when dealing with situations that require an approach.
- **Managing Indecisiveness;** Geminis often struggle with making decisions due to their many interests. To address this challenge they should strive to make informed choices and stick to them by setting deadlines for decision making.

- **Deepening Emotional Connections**; While Geminis excel at surface level interactions they could work on forging deeper connections. This can be accomplished through honest communication well as investing quality time in meaningful conversations.

- **Balancing Enthusiasm with Realism**; Geminis naturally possess enthusiasm but sometimes lean towards excessive optimism. It is crucial for them to strike a balance between enthusiasm and realism particularly when it comes to planning and executing tasks.

In conclusion individuals born under the sign of Gemini can maximize their potential by embracing their communication skills, adaptability, curiosity and sociable nature. To overcome their weaknesses they should work on being consistent. They can develop patience and decisiveness, nurturing depth and finding a balance between enthusiasm and realism. By doing this Geminis can tap into their talents and also experience personal growth. Overall they can achieve a well rounded and satisfying life.

As we wrap up this exploration of the self improvement journey undertaken by individuals born under the Gemini zodiac sign it becomes evident that the path they traverse is as diverse and dynamic, as their nature. By embracing their qualities and harnessing their strengths Geminis can unlock a realm of possibilities in both their professional lives.

The future looks promising for Geminis when it comes to self improvement. They have an ability to adapt, think quickly and communicate effectively which positions them for success, in many aspects of life. By embracing the exercises and techniques outlined in this chapter, they can make use of their strengths and overcome challenges. Naturally this will lead to a more satisfying and balanced life.

Remember that the journey of self improvement for Geminis is ongoing and ever evolving. As they learn to balance their nature, embrace their curiosity and channel their energies productively they open themselves up to many possibilities. The key is to remain receptive to change and growth while allowing their inherent talents to flourish. At the same time, continuously work on areas that need improvement.

In summary the path towards self improvement for Geminis involves finding harmony within their contrasting characteristics and leveraging their versatility as a strength.

By committing themselves to growth and being open minded to explore alternative approaches Geminis can develop remarkable self awareness and find fulfillment in their journey. The future holds huge potential, for those who embrace this path guiding them towards an enriched life.

CHAPTER 6:
THE YEAR AHEAD

As the alignment of stars begins a new cycle, in the zodiac individuals born under the sign of Gemini find themselves on the brink of a year filled with possibilities. Renowned for their intellect, adaptability and strong communication skills, Geminis are poised to navigate through aspects of life that will require these qualities. This chapter aims to unravel the tapestry that awaits those who belong to this sign. By combining foresight with advice we will embark on a journey through key astrological events that are destined to influence Gemini's love life and relationships, career, finances, health and much more.

From Mercury's retrogrades (as it's their ruling planet) to Venus and Jupiter's transits, each movement of these celestial bodies carries its own significance that will shape Gemini's experiences and opportunities. We will explore how these cosmic shifts can impact their lives. Throughout each section we delve into here, Geminis will gain insights on how to harness the influences brought by these celestial forces. They will also learn how to navigate any challenges that may arise.

Overall our goal in this chapter is to equip Geminis with the tools and knowledge to make the most out of the year ahead. So join us as we embark on a journey through the year for Geminis. A year filled with opportunities for growth, self discovery and a deeper understanding of how the cosmic forces influence their daily lives.

A YEARLY HOROSCOPE GUIDE FOR GEMINI

When it comes to creating a horoscope guide, for Gemini individuals the focus lies in providing insights and forecasts for various aspects of their life such as career, relationships, personal growth and health. It's important to remember that while astrology can offer some guidance and entertainment value it shouldn't be seen as a substitute for advice in any field. Here's a general outline for a horoscope guide specifically tailored to Geminis.

FINANCES

- **Start of the Year;** The beginning of the year will place emphasis on career development. There may be chances for advancement or taking on new projects. From a financial perspective it's wise to plan and budget accordingly for the changes.
- **Mid Year;** The middle of the year could bring some challenges. However by staying adaptable and utilizing your communication skills effectively you'll be able to navigate through them. This period also presents opportunities for networking and exploring career paths.
- **End of Year;** As the year draws to a close all your hard work will start paying off. You might receive recognition. Even you could find yourself on the path, towards promotion. Financial

stability is on the rise creating conditions for investments or major purchases.

RELATIONSHIPS AND SOCIAL LIFE

- **Start of the Year**; The beginning of the year brings opportunities for new connections and friendships. For those currently in relationships effective communication plays an important role during this period.
- **Mid Year**; The middle of the year may bring some misunderstandings in relationships. It's important to maintain openness and honesty in your communication. Singles might find this a unique time to explore romantic interests.

- **End of Year;** As the year comes to an end, harmony prevails in your relationships. It's a time to deepen bonds and reconnect with loved ones. Social gatherings and celebrations take center stage.

PERSONAL GROWTH AND HEALTH

- **Start of the Year;** The start of the year focuses on development. It presents an opportunity for Geminis to acquire skills or engage in hobbies. In terms of health, maintaining a balanced lifestyle is key.
- **Mid Year;** The middle of the year calls for self reflection. It's a period to reassess goals and aspirations. Prioritizing well being becomes crucial during this time; practices such as meditation or yoga can be beneficial.
- **End of Year;** As the year draws to an end you will experience renewed purpose and clarity. Maintaining health is important so make sure to not overlook check ups.

TRAVEL AND EXPLORATION

- **Throughout the Year;** There are many travel opportunities available, at different times throughout the year. Overall it's more favorable to go on short trips rather than long journeys. These short trips can offer both relaxation and opportunities for growth.

In conclusion for Gemini individuals this year will bring chances for professional development alongside challenges that will test and enhance your abilities. Being adaptable, communicative and open, to learning will be skills to navigate this year successfully. Embrace the changes that come your way. You'll find it to be a fulfilling journey.

KEY ASTROLOGICAL EVENTS AND THEIR IMPACT ON GEMINI

Different zodiac signs can be influenced in various ways by key astrological events. In the case of Gemini individuals, specific astrological occurrences throughout the year can have an impact on aspects of their lives including emotions and decision making processes. Here's an overview of some key astrological events and how they might affect Gemini.

Mercury Retrograde

- Impact; Since Mercury is the ruling planet for Gemini its retrograde periods can have a significant influence on them. During these times communication issues, misunderstandings and travel disruptions are common. Geminis may also experience a reflective state.
- Advice; It's advisable for Geminis to double check all forms of communication. Avoid initiating projects during Mercury retrograde. It's also an opportunity to revisit and revise projects.

Solar and Lunar Eclipses

- Impact; Eclipses often bring about changes and revelations. For Gemini individuals solar eclipses can signal beginnings in areas such as growth and relationships while lunar eclipses may bring closure or emotional climaxes.
- Advice; Embrace the changes brought about by eclipses. Solar eclipses present circumstances for Geminis to embark on ventures or foster relationships while lunar eclipses are ideal moments to let go of what no longer serves them.

Venus Transit

- Impact; Venus governs love and finance; thus its transit can affect Gemini's relationships and financial matters.
- Advice; During this time Geminis often find clarity in their relationships. May feel compelled to reevaluate their strategies. My advice would be to focus on maintaining balance in your budget

and being open and honest with your loved ones.
It's an opportunity for Geminis to resolve any
lingering conflicts with those to them.

Mars Transit

- Impact; The transit of Mars can have an impact
  on energy levels and ambition for Geminis. It has
  the potential to enhance drive in career related
  endeavors and physical activities.
- Advice; Be cautious of impulsiveness or getting
  into conflicts. Make use of this energy by
  pursuing goals and engaging in physical activities
  that bring you fulfillment.

Jupiter's Transit

- Impact; Jupiter's transit can bring about luck and
  expansion for Geminis. It opens doors for
  growth and abundance in areas of life such as
  career, education and travel opportunities.
- Advice; seize these chances for development by
  exploring education options, embarking on
  exciting travels or considering expanding your
  professional horizons.

Saturn's Transit

- Impact; Saturn's transit is known for its influence
  on structure and discipline. During this period
  Geminis might face increased responsibilities
  along with lessons in the realms of career growth
  and personal development.
- Advice; Stay disciplined, focused and embrace the
  challenges that come your way. This is a time

when Geminis need to put in work and stay
determined as it holds the promise of long term
rewards.

New Moon and Full Moon

- Impact; During the New Moon and Full Moon
  phases Geminis can experience noticeable
  impacts. The New Moon can inspire them to
  embark on projects or make changes in their
  lifestyles. On the other hand the Full Moon may
  bring about a culmination or fulfillment of
  aspects of their lives.

- Advice; Utilize the energy of the New Moon for
  setting intentions and starting endeavors. As for
  the Full Moon it's a time for self reflection.
  Witnessing the results of your efforts. By staying
  aware of these events and understanding their
  effects Geminis can navigate through life more
  smoothly while making use of any opportunities
  that come their way.

KEY AREAS OF INTEREST

LOVE AND RELATIONSHIPS

The impact of astrology on the love life of Gemini
individuals is set to bring changes in the year. Important
astrological events, such as the movement of Venus and
Mars will play key roles.

Venus, known as the planet of love, will enter a
position that enhances Geminis charm and social skills.
This period creates conditions for forming connections or

strengthening existing relationships. Geminis will feel more open to love and establishing bonds.

When Mars influences Gemini's love life there may be a surge of passion and impulsive behavior. It is important for Geminis to navigate this time carefully in order to avoid conflicts within their relationships.

Mercury, which governs Gemini, goes retrograde periodically. During these phases misunderstandings or communication issues might arise within relationships. It is crucial for Geminis to practice patience and ensure communication during this time.

Strategies for Love and Relationships

- **Open Communication;** During Mercury retrograde periods it is vital for Geminis to prioritize honest communication in order to prevent misunderstandings.
- **Embrace Romantic Opportunities;** The transit of Venus presents an opportunity for Geminis to explore romantic possibilities or rekindle existing relationships.
- **Managing Impulsiveness;** During the time when Marss, in transit Geminis need to be mindful of their nature when it comes to matters of the heart.

CAREER AND FINANCES

Gemini's financial aspects will be influenced by planetary movements this year. The movement of Jupiter, the planet associated with expansion bondicates growth and opportunities in career and finances. This period is favorable for advancing in one's job and making investments. Then, Saturn's movement might bring about challenges and increased responsibilities at work requiring Geminis to practice discipline and hard work.

Career and Financial Strategies

- **Seizing Opportunities**; Make use of the period when Jupiter is in transit to broaden your career prospects and explore avenues for growth.
- **Maintaining Discipline;** During Saturn's transit focus on long term goals. Stay disciplined to overcome any obstacles that may arise.

HEALTH AND WELLNESS

Gemini's well being will be subtly influenced by movements throughout the year. Lunar cycles during the New Moon and Full Moon phases can have an impact on Gemini's emotional well being as well as physical health. These periods call for self care practices that help maintain balance.

Advice on Health and Well being

- **Achieving Physical Balance;** Incorporate the cycles into your focus on emotional well being and physical health. Engage in practices such as meditation and regular exercise as they can have effects.
- **Regular Health Check ups;** It is advisable to undergo health check ups to keep track of your well being.

PERSONAL GROWTH AND SELF DISCOVERY

The astrological events throughout the year provide opportunities for personal growth and self discovery especially for individuals born under the Gemini zodiac sign. Mercury Retrograde periods are ideal for introspection reflecting on goals and reevaluating them. During Jupiter and Saturn Transits, expand your knowledge and skills. Be sure to also incorporate discipline and structure into your growth endeavors.

Strategies for Personal Growth

- **Reflecting and Reevaluating**; Take advantage of the energy during Mercury retrograde to engage in self reflection and set goals.
- **Embrace Learning;** The transit of Jupiter presents an opportunity to pursue pursuits or develop new skills.
- **Develop Discipline;** Utilize Saturn's influence to establish discipline in activities related to self improvement.

By understanding these influences and aligning with them Gemini individuals can navigate the year with greater awareness and purpose. This will allow them to make the most of opportunities for growth in areas such, as love, career, health and personal development.

As we wrap up our exploration of what lies for Gemini in the year it's evident that the upcoming months will present a mix of challenges, opportunities and significant moments of growth. With Gemini's diverse nature and the unique influences, from the realm we can expect a dynamic and diverse year that reflects the essence of this zodiac sign.

It is important for Geminis to embrace the journey that awaits them with a balanced mind and adaptability. The astrological events throughout the year will require a balance between flexibility and decisiveness as Geminis navigate through both sailing and rough waters. Whether it pertains to matters of love and relationships, career and finances, health and well being or personal growth and self discovery, every aspect offers an opportunity for learning and evolution.

The key to making the most out of this year lies in harnessing your strengths as a Gemini. Your intellectual curiosity, communication skills and ability to adapt will be your assets. By staying attuned to cues while remaining true, to your nature you can transform challenges into stepping stones towards success.

Amidst all the whirlwind activities and changes that may come your way this year it is crucial for Geminis to find moments of stillness and grounding. Remember to find time for recovery practices such as spending quality time in nature or pursuing your hobbies. These activities will help you maintain a sense of balance and well being in your paced life throughout the year.

When looking ahead keep in mind that every experience you encounter whether positive or challenging presents an opportunity for growth. The astrological events occurring this year are not cosmic happenings but rather serve as guides pointing you towards a deeper understanding of yourself and your role in the world.

To sum it up, the upcoming year holds a multitude of possibilities for Gemini individuals to explore and embrace through their actions, decisions and attitudes. Embrace your Gemini traits, like enthusiasm and adaptability as you venture forth into this chapter. You'll discover that the year has much to offer in terms of enriching the tapestry of your life. Stay open minded, keep a heart and allow the stars to guide you on a journey of self discovery and fulfillment.

CHAPTER 7:
FAMOUS "GEMINI" PERSONALITIES

This chapter celebrates the lives and accomplishments of famous individuals who were born under the sign of Gemini. From leaders and visionaries, to artists and entertainers we can observe how being a Gemini has influenced their journeys by instilling them with adaptability, eloquence and an insatiable thirst for knowledge. Each person we encounter in this section offers us a fresh perspective into the essence of Gemini. A combination of complexity, creativity and an unwavering pursuit of expression and comprehension.

The individuals featured here have made significant contributions to their respective fields and also embody various aspects of Gemini traits. Whether it's in politics, artistry, science or entertainment their stories serve as evidence to the nature of Gemini. As we explore the lives of these known individuals we gain insights into how their dual nature can lead to remarkable accomplishments. Their stories serve as inspiration showcasing how the traits associated with Gemini can be channeled towards achieving greatness, exerting influence and leaving a legacy. Come along as we pay tribute to these Gemini personalities who have made a lasting impact on our world. They truly embody the essence of the Gemini spirit.

- Date of Birth: June 14 1946.

- Brief Biography: Donald Trump is a businessman, television personality and politician who served as the President of the United States.

- Gemini Traits: Trump is known for his ability to communicate effectively and sometimes controversially showcasing the persuasive qualities associated with Gemini.

- Impact: As a figure in business and a polarizing political leader he has made an impact on American politics and international relations.

- Personal Life: Trump's personal life, including his marriages and large family has received considerable media attention.

PAUL MCCARTNEY

- Date of Birth: June 18 1942.
- Brief Biography: Sir Paul McCartney is a musician who was part of The Beatles and later achieved great success as a solo artist.
- Gemini Traits: McCartneys versatility in music styles and his engaging communication skills highlight his adaptability as a Gemini.
- Impact: He has had an impact on the music industry influencing generations of musicians and fans alike.
- Personal Life: Besides his career, McCartneys activism and philanthropy have played a role in shaping his public image.

MARILYN MONROE

- Date of Birth: June 1 1926.
- Brief Biography: Marilyn Monroe, the known actress, model and singer gained fame for her portrayal of comedic "blonde bombshell" characters.
- Gemini Traits: Her versatility, as an actress and her charismatic personality are a reflection of the traits often associated with Gemini.
- Impact: Monroe's impact on culture was significant as she became a sex symbol and left an enduring legacy in the entertainment industry. Additionally
- Personal Life: Her personal life and tragic death have captivated interest for years.

QUEEN VICTORIA

- Date of Birth: May 24 1819.

- Brief Biography: Queen Victoria held the title of Queen of the United Kingdom of Great Britain and Ireland. She also served as Empress of India during her reign.

- Gemini Traits: Known for her communication skills and adaptability to changing times she exemplified traits commonly associated with Gemini.

- Impact: Queen Victoria's influence extended beyond her reign; she made a lasting impact on politics, culture. Even shaped the image of the monarchy.

- Personal Life: her marriage to Prince Albert and her extended period of mourning following his passing were aspects of her life.

CLINT EASTWOOD

- Date of Birth: May 31st in 1930.

- Brief Biography: Clint Eastwood is widely recognized for his roles in films that showcase his ability to adapt effortlessly to characters.

- Gemini Traits: As a director he exhibits communication skills that align with the traits frequently attributed to Gemini individuals.

- Impact: Eastwood has made an impact in the film industry both through his acting and directing work.

- Personal Life: His personal life, including his involvement in politics and relationships has garnered attention.

ANNE FRANK

- Date of Birth: June 12, 1929.
- Brief Biography: She was a diarist of Jewish heritage who gained fame for her diary chronicling her experiences during the Holocaust.
- Gemini Traits: In her diary she showcased Gemini qualities through writing and expressive communication.
- Impact: Anne Frank's diary has had an effect on shaping how the world perceives the Holocaust and stands as a piece of historical literature.
- Personal Life: Her life in hiding and tragic death in a concentration camp are central to her story.

TUPAC SHAKUR

- Date of Birth: June 16, 1971.
- Brief Biography: Tupac Shakur was a rapper and actor who gained recognition for addressing contemporary social issues through his music.
- Gemini Traits: Tupac's versatility, as an artist and his eloquent and straightforward communication style reflect Gemini characteristics.
- Impact: Tupac Shakur is widely regarded as one of the rappers of all time with his influence continuing to resonate within the hip hop industry.

- Personal Life: The public is still fascinated by his life, which includes his involvement in the East Coast West Coast hip hop rivalry and his unfortunate death.

JOHNNY DEPP

- Date of Birth: June 9 1963.
- Brief Biography: Johnny Depp is an actor and producer renowned for his diverse film choices.
- Gemini Traits: Depp's ability to effortlessly portray a range of characters throughout his acting career truly showcases the versatility often associated with Geminis.
- Impact: With his acting style he has undoubtedly left a mark on the film industry.
- Personal Life: The media has extensively covered Depp's life, including his relationships and legal battles.

KYLIE MINOGUE

- Date of Birth: May 28 1968.
- Brief Biography: Kylie Minogue is a singer, songwriter and actress known for her pop music career and unforgettable hits like "Can't Get You Out of My Head."
- Gemini Traits: Minogues talent for adapting to music styles and her captivating stage presence perfectly exemplify the qualities typically associated with Gemini individuals.

- Impact: Minogue has undeniably made an impact on the pop music scene. Rightfully earned her status as a pop icon.
- Personal Life: known for keeping her personal life private, despite occasional media spotlight on her relationships and health challenges.

ANGELINA JOLIE

- Date of Birth: June 4 1975.
- Brief Biography: Angelina Jolie is an actress, filmmaker and humanitarian known for her work both on and off the screen.
- Gemini Traits: Jolies talent as an actress and her effective communication skills align with the characteristics often associated with Geminis.
- Impact: She has made an impact in the film industry. Has been highly recognized for her humanitarian endeavors.
- Personal Life: Her marriages, family life and dedication to work have garnered attention from the public.

TIM BERNERS LEE

- Date of Birth: June 8 1955.
- Brief Biography: Sir Tim Berners Lee is an engineer and computer scientist who is best known as the creator of the World Wide Web.
- Gemini Traits: Berners Lee's thinking and ability to explain complex ideas in simple terms exemplify qualities often attributed to Geminis.
- Impact: His invention has fundamentally transformed how people access and share information worldwide.
- Personal Life: Although he maintains a low profile in public his contributions to technology and advocacy for an open internet are noteworthy.

ALANIS MORISSETTE

- Date of Birth: June 1 1974.
- Brief Biography: Alanis Nadine Morissette is a Canadian and American singer and songwriter. She is widely recognized for her mezzo soprano vocals and thought provoking lyrics.
- Gemini Traits: Explores various musical styles—a characteristic that resonates with Gemini traits.
- Impact: Alanis Morissette has made an impact on the music industry with her album "Jagged Little Pill" being particularly influential.
- Personal Life: Apart from her achievements she has also been open about her journey, in spirituality and mental health which has become an integral part of her public narrative.

As we come to the end of our exploration into the lives and legacies of these Gemini individuals we are left with a tapestry that beautifully captures the essence of the Gemini spirit. This journey, through Geminis from many walks of life has not only given us a glimpse into their remarkable accomplishments but has also showcased the unique characteristics that define the Gemini zodiac sign.

The stories of these individuals highlight the diversity and adaptability in Geminis. From artists like Marilyn Monroe and Johnny Depp who embody genius to figures like Donald Trump and Queen Victoria, known for their leadership each person exemplifies the dynamic and multifaceted nature of Gemini. Overall they demonstrate how Geminis can channel their curiosity, communication skills and adaptability across fields leaving an indelible impact on the world.

These profiles remind us of the potential that comes with embracing Gemini qualities such as versatility and intellectual agility. They show us that a Geminis ability to perceive things from new perspectives can be a tool for innovation and influence. The lives of these individuals also highlight how important it is to find balance between Gemini's duality of introspection and extroversion.

For those born under the Gemini zodiac sign these stories provide inspiration and a sense of connection. They demonstrate what Geminis can accomplish when they embrace their abilities and approach life with an open mind and adaptable attitude. The achievements of these Geminis can serve as a force encouraging current and future Geminis to pursue their passions and utilize their unique talents to leave a lasting impact. As we conclude this chapter we are reminded that the journey of a Gemini is one defined by exploration, learning and self expression. It is an expedition that encompasses diversity and leaves us in awe of all the personalities we have delved into.

CONCLUSION

Finally we have reached the conclusion of this book. As we conclude our exploration of the world of the Gemini zodiac sign we find ourselves at a moment of introspection and synthesis. This book has taken us through the landscape of Geminis essence from its mythological origins, to its impact on personal and professional aspects. In this conclusion our goal is to bring the diverse facets of the Gemini experience together to provide a cohesive summary and a reflective ending to this enlightening journey. Now let's explore the key points, summarized about Gemini in the previous chapters.

- **Chapter 1. History and Mythology;** Here we delved into how history and mythology have shaped our understanding of Gemini. We explored how ancient stories continue to influence our perception of this zodiac sign. We also highlighted the symbolism of duality and communication skills in Gemini.

- **Chapter 2. Love & Compatibility;** This chapter explored how Geminis approach love and relationships. It revealed their desire for connection with partners who're good communicators and a yearning for a dynamic yet harmonious companionship.

- **Chapter 3. Friends and Family;** In this chapter we examined the dynamics that surround Geminis family and friends. We revealed their adaptability, versatility as well as their emphasis on intellectual bonds, within personal relationships.

- **Chapter 4. Career and Finances;** In this chapter we delved into the career and financial realm of Geminis. This highlighted their inclination towards careers that offer stimulation, creativity and ample opportunities for communication. Additionally we explored their approach to financial matters.

- **Chapter 5. Personal Growth;** In this chapter we extensively discussed the journey of self improvement for Geminis. We emphasized the importance of striking a balance between their ranging interests and personal development. Furthermore we underscored how embracing their versatility and adaptability contributes to their self improvement.

- **Chapter 6. The Year Ahead;** In this chapter we explored astrological forecasts tailored to Geminis. These forecasts provided insights on how they can navigate challenges and seize opportunities across various aspects of life in the year ahead.

- **Chapter 7. Famous Gemini Personalities;** This chapter is dedicated to commemorating individuals who embody the traits associated with the Gemini sign. It serves as a showcase of the impact and diversity displayed by Geminis throughout history.

As we come to the end it's clear that the Gemini zodiac sign is all about duality, curiosity and adaptability. This book has shed light on the diverse nature of those born under this sign. Geminis are encouraged to embrace their unique qualities. Their communication skills, their ability to adapt to new situations and their varied interests. This book serves not just as a wealth of knowledge about Geminis but as a starting point for them to navigate their lives with a deeper understanding of their astrological identity.

In summary this enlightening exploration has taken us through the world that defines what it means to be a Gemini. Throughout the book we have delved into aspects of Gemini individuals ranging from the way they navigate love, friendship, careers and more. Our goal has been to provide readers with an understanding of the complexities and intellectual depth that define a Gemini.

By peeling back the layers of this multifaceted sign we have shed light on their characteristics, challenges and strengths. Through these chapters readers can discover a reflection of themselves. Furthermore they can gain valuable insights on how to embrace their unique qualities. A key takeaway from our exploration is the celebration of Geminis duality as a source of strength. In addition to their ability to adapt and communicate effectively. Forging connections on deep levels is not merely a trait but a remarkable power that aids them in navigating the intricacies of today's world.

Remember that astrology goes beyond uncovering personality traits; it offers us a lens through which we can comprehend our interactions, motivations and life paths. By acknowledging the significance of influences like those observed in Gemini individuals we gain an appreciation for the diversity and richness that characterizes our experiences.

Attention all Gemini individuals; Embrace your energy and intellectual curiosity as they are defining qualities that make you who you are. Your adaptability should not be seen as indecision. Rather, as a testament to your potential. Utilize your communication skills to bridge gaps. Let your curiosity guide you towards new territories and allow your versatility to navigate life's ever changing circumstances.

The world is full of possibilities and Geminis have the abilities to paint their own journeys. One with vibrant colors through innovation, relationships and personal growth. Embrace your duality, cherish your communication skills and thrive in your adaptability. These are the strengths that make you as a Gemini truly remarkable.

Best wishes to you Gemini!

www.ingramcontent.com/pod-product-compliance
Lightning Source LLC
Chambersburg PA
CBHW061334120726

48001CB00002B/849